Lina Hultin,
anything is possible so dream big!

Gloria Riherd

Never give up!

BECKY HAMMON
Shooting for Success

By Gloria Riherd

Gloria Riherd

Dedication: To all girls in sports everywhere
—GR

Text copyright © 2018
by Gloria Riherd
Edited by Joanna Jones,
Jones Literature LLC.
Cover and internal design © 2018
by Chicken Creek Communications
All rights reserved.
Distributed by Gloria Riherd
Contact the author at riherglo@netscape.net
Photos reprinted with permission from the NBA.
Photos page 10 reprinted with permission from Colorado State University.
Photos page 14 reprinted with permission from MSG Photo Services.
Printed by Chicken Creek Communications, LLC, Spearfish, SD
First Edition, 2018

Library of Congress Cataloging-in-Publication Data
Riherd, Gloria
  Becky Hammon: Shooting for Success/Gloria Riherd; foreword by Becky Hammon. – 1st ed. (36) p.
  Summary: Women's basketball star Becky Hammon demonstrates strong leadership skills, determination and self confidence to accomplish her goals.
  ISBN: 978- 0-9973849-3-2
  (1. Hammon, Becky, 1977- — Juvenile literature. 2. Women basketball players – United States – Biography – Juvenile literature. 3. Basketball players – United States – Biography – Juvenile literature.)
  I. Title.
796.323/092 Hammon 2018 (DDC23)
(Biography)
GV884.H366 R54 2018

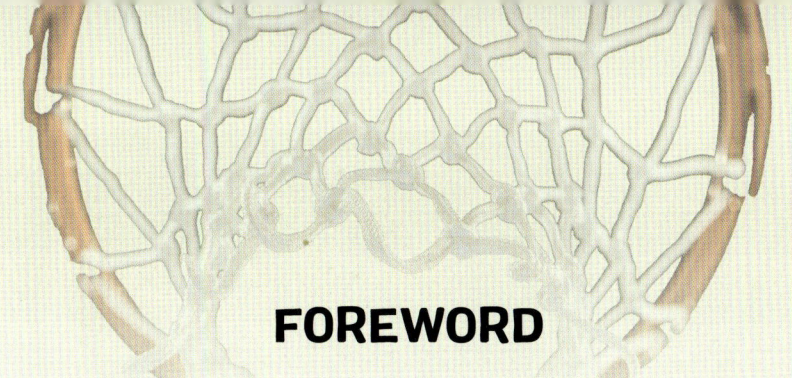

FOREWORD

To the young people of my home state of South Dakota:

My early years probably didn't start out so different from yours. I, like yourself, grew up in the beautiful Black Hills. Not only did I fall in love with the outdoors, but I also fell in love with the game of basketball. It's my first true love.

As Mrs. Riherd chronicles my journey throughout this book, I know she could probably give you many first-hand accounts of me playing basketball, or me going on softball trips, or maybe even some stories of spaghetti dinners at Coach Riherd's house! Coach Riherd was one of the first people to invest countless hours in teaching me the game of basketball, and demanding excellence from me both as a player, teammate, and young woman.

I started playing basketball for one simple reason: it was fun! I hope that whatever you are passionate about, whether it be basketball, music, dance, or whatever, that you work at it with 100 percent focus and determination – and don't forget to have fun! Strive to be great, believe you can be great, and put people in and around your life that will help you achieve your goals. I certainly didn't get to where I am today without the help of many committed coaches, teammates, family,

Becky's first true love was playing basketball

and friends both cheering me on, and also picking me up after being knocked to the ground either mentally, physically, or in some instance ... when life was just unfair. But guess what? Life has failures, disappointments, injuries, and injustices for all of us at some time or another. BUT what matters most is how YOU respond to these situations. My response was always to get back up, and try again and again until I got it right!! When a door of opportunity was closed to me, I would look for a window to crawl through instead!

I hope this book inspires you to be great. I hope it conveys to you that you are special and have your own unique journey that begins with new choices and opportunities every morning. I hope you see, that at the end of the day, you are not so different than me!! My journey led me to be a professional basketball player for 16 years and to be the first full-time female assistant coach in the NBA or in any of the other four major sports leagues in America.

Where will your journey take you? Decide to BE YOU and BE GREAT!

God Bless,
Coach Becky Hammon

Becky Hammon's high school senior picture

Becky was born on March 11, 1977, in Rapid City, South Dakota. As a little girl she enjoyed playing basketball in the backyard with her older brother, Matt, and his friends. "We played 2 on 2, or 3 on 3 for countless hours," said Becky.

Her dad was the first one to teach her the fundamentals of ball handling, dribbling, and passing. He taught her how to be a leader on the court. Because she was smaller than the other players, he gave her advice that has always stuck with her: "Don't try to be in the air too much. Just be on the ground and rule the ground."

Becky wanted to prove that she was just as good as the boys. Her mom soon nicknamed her "Bubba" because she worked so hard. "My mom was instrumental in giving me an overall confidence and strength inside myself. She's been my biggest cheerleader!"

Fans cheering for Bubba, their favorite player

At Stevens High School in Rapid City, SD, many people could not imagine that Becky would be so successful. After all, she was only 5' 6" which is not tall for being a girls basketball player. Going against other taller players certainly added an additional challenge for Becky. She made up her mind early on that she was going to have to be quicker, faster and smarter than her opponents. Because of her positive attitude, "Bubba" became very popular. She was a good role model for demonstrating leadership skills, determination, and self confidence.

Teammate Jody Riherd, Coach Riherd, and Becky

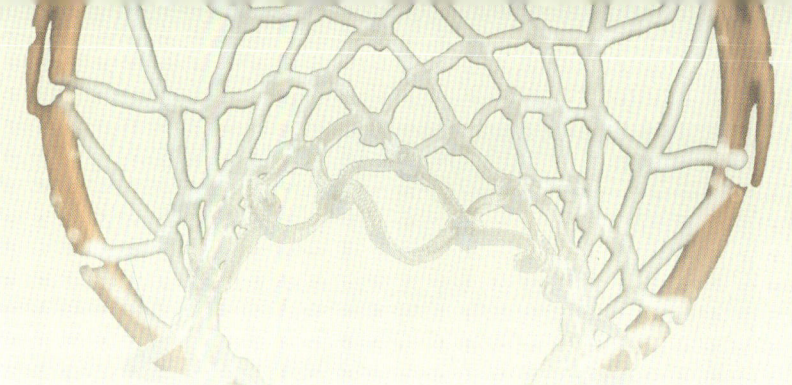

Her high school coach, Ron Riherd, was a stickler on learning the fundamentals of basketball. Becky felt Coach Riherd was instrumental in her success as a shooter. He said, "Becky was the first one on the court and the last one to leave after practice. She always wanted to know more about the game."

Ron described a situation in which Rapid City Stevens was playing their rival Rapid City Central. In an uncharacteristic way, Becky fouled out with only a couple minutes left to play. Stevens ended up losing the game by a couple points.

Entering the locker room, before Coach Riherd had a chance to address the team, Becky stood up and started talking to her teammates. She said they were a good team and needed to play with more confidence. Becky was always a great basketball player and team leader.

She earned a varsity letter in girls basketball in all four years of high school. After averaging 26 points per game as a senior, she was voted by the South Dakota Basketball Coaches Association as the South Dakota Player of the Year.

Playing for Colorado State University

　　Becky went on to play at Colorado State University. Many people thought that being only 5' 6" she would have difficulties amongst some of the very tall girl basketball players, everyone except Becky. "I was always smaller and slower than everybody else, so I had to figure out other ways to be successful," she said. "Some people can survive on their athleticism; I had to survive on my brain." At Colorado State University, she earned Women's College All-American player and Colorado's Sportswoman of the Year awards.

　　It seemed as though she couldn't be stopped. She set many records which led to her being inducted into the Colorado State University Sports Hall of Fame and the Colorado Sports Hall of Fame.

Scoring for the New York Liberty

As a graduating senior, players are either drafted (chosen) or invited to try out for a league team as a free agent. Despite all of her accolades, she was not drafted as a professional basketball player in the Women's National Basketball Association (WNBA).

The coach for the New York Liberty saw something great in Becky Hammon and asked her to try out for the team as a walk-on. "I was the last person picked to sit on the Liberty bench," Becky said. "I had to work hard to improve every year because I wanted more than to just be on the bench."

She soon became a fan favorite in New York. Becky proved to be even better than anyone ever imagined.

Suffering injuries became part of the game

Becky's success did not come easily. She suffered many injuries during her 16-year professional career. She had anterior cruciate ligament (ACL) surgery on both knees. The ACL is the most commonly injured ligament in the knee. People often tear the ACL by changing direction rapidly, slowing down from running, or landing from a jump. Once the ACL is torn, the knee usually becomes unstable and surgery is required. The ACL surgeries cost her a significant loss of time during two separate seasons.

Becky was plagued with plantar fasciitis which is pain in the heels of her feet. This is caused from straining the ligament that supports the arch. Other injuries included a shoulder strain, a broken finger, and numerous other sprains. Becky continued to play through most of her injuries.

But if you asked Becky about her injuries, she would only downplay their significance. In fact, she is quick to say how all good and bad experiences shaped her into what she is today.

Directing her San Antonio teammates

During the 2007 season, Becky was traded to the San Antonio Silver Stars. "From the first day I stepped into Texas, everyone made me feel honored to put on a Stars uniform." She continued to be a strong player and leader for her new team. At San Antonio, she earned another nickname from her fans, "Big Shot Becky" because of her ability to score points in clutch moments.

"Becky Hammon has made a lasting mark on the San Antonio Stars and the WNBA," said Coach Hughes. "She has worked tirelessly to become the best she could be on and off the court. She has inspired in a wonderful way. The beauty of her game has been an amazing thing in which to have a front row seat."

Becky won an Olympic bronze medal

Becky always aspired to play in the Olympics. Becky and her agent sent a letter to the Olympic selection committee and coaches asking if she could be selected to try out for the USA Olympic team. Not one member responded to their request.

She then received an invitation to play for Russia in the 2008 Olympics because that was the country where she was playing during the WNBA off-season. "I can sit in my apartment and wish I could play or I can play for Russia," said Becky. After much agonizing over the decision, Hammon announced she would join the Russian national team, fulfilling her lifelong dream to compete in the Olympics.

Russia lost to the United States in the semifinals, but she helped the Russian team to win a bronze medal by scoring 22 points against China. "The medal is nice and it was unbelievable to be on that podium," she said, "but … it was all about the journey to get there." She continued to be positive, continued to encourage her teammates, and always was the hardest worker.

Showing determination and persistence

No matter what team she played for, she had the integrity to play basketball to the best of her ability. On a typical game day in San Antonio, she went to practice for two to three hours in the morning, then to the gym to work out. After a short break, she would head back to the arena around 4 p.m. where she stayed until about 11 p.m.

"I've had to overcome many obstacles to be where I am today. Honestly, I wouldn't change a thing. Being short, or not from the 'right school,' not having the 'right build,' not being athletic enough, etc. There's a long list people had for me not to be successful. But all those factors combined instilled into my fiber how to work hard, have a strong work ethic, and to utilize persistence, patience, determination, resilience and craftiness. I learned how to make others around me better, to be a giver and not a taker. I learned how to work together with people and how to serve people. Integrity ... in essence, is what built my character."

Shooting jump shots with perfect form

When asked to compare men and women basketball players, Becky said, "I think men and women work equally hard and should be equally respected for the work and time they've put in. I think athletes are athletes, whether male or female. Athletes want to be pushed and taught how to become the best that they can be. I think someone who truly understands the game of basketball can really appreciate the way women play just as much as the men."

She also found that the mental aspects of the game were at least as important as the physical ones. "I don't care if you're a man or a woman," she said. "The best thing about Michael Jordan was his mind for the game."

Playing in the Olympics in Beijing was a career highlight

Besides playing in her WNBA regular season, she has traveled all over the world playing basketball in Russia, Italy, Israel, England and China. The Rapid City native counts winning a bronze medal at the 2008 Summer Olympic Games in Beijing, China as one of her career highlights.

In honor of her success, she chose to give back to others in need. She began a worldwide fan club known as the "Hammonites," which covers the world – the United States, Canada, China, Brazil, Belgium, Russia and other countries. Each year the Hammonites, in honor of her birthday, donate money which she matches and then passes on to a battered women and children's shelter in San Antonio, Texas. She also donated to the International Medical Corps to facilitate efforts in the Haiti earthquake recovery.

Making blind passes led to many assists

"After 16 years as a WNBA veteran, I am grateful for everyone that has helped me along the way." Becky retired in 2014 at the age of 37. Hammon was the all-time leader in assists, points per game, and three-point shots made. Becky Hammon was a six-time All Star selection who ranked seventh in WNBA history in total points (5,756), second in three-point field goals made (817), fourth in assists (1,663), sixth in games played (440) and first in free throw percentage (89.7 percent).

Driving hard to the basket

In the history of the WNBA, Becky was named one of the top 20 players. WNBA president Laurel Richie exclaimed, "Becky epitomizes what the WNBA is all about: she has truly shown the world what is possible. Having gone undrafted in 1999, she was determined to make her dream come true. Hard work and talent got her noticed and earned her a spot on the roster, and she never looked back. In addition to all her accomplishments, her feisty leadership and no-look passes have made her a fan favorite. We thank Becky for her accomplishments to the growth of this wonderful game, and we wish her all the best on her future endeavors."

An honor to be the first NBA woman coach!

Becky Hammon has already made history multiple times during her basketball career. However, she continues to amaze and surprise everyone. She is now the first National Basketball Association (NBA) assistant female coach for the San Antonio Spurs. Becky also won a Las Vegas Summer League title in 2015, becoming the first woman to be the head coach of an NBA summer league team. This is a testament of Becky's basketball knowledge and skill. She doesn't dwell on being one of the few women coaches in the NBA. "At the end of the day, my being a woman really has nothing to do with it," she says.

Becky Hammon is highly respected among the WNBA and NBA leagues. People who know Becky, understand she always puts herself in positions to create opportunities. "Hope and encouragement, especially hope, is probably one of the greatest things you can give another person," she said. "I mean, what a gift to allow that person to be able to dream, to be able to say, why not me? Why couldn't I be the first?" We can only wonder what more Becky Hammon will accomplish in the future.

Having fun along her life's journey

"I know what both ends of success feel like. I think my journey has given me a lot of perspective. It is all about overcoming obstacles. I've been the last person on the bench, the last one to be picked on a team, and I have also been an All Star starter. My life in basketball has taught me to be so thankful for every opportunity and to treat people from all different walks of life with respect and dignity."

As a professional basketball player, does she miss playing basketball herself? "I don't think you ever lose the desire to play basketball. I miss it so much! I try not to think about it," she said. Although she loves coaching, she still thinks of herself as a player.

Becky Hammon was a basketball player for as long as she can remember. Becky was not tall in stature, but she stood tall in the hearts of all her fans. It was not always easy, but, by not giving up, she found success at every level.

"There's really no magic remedy, if you want to be good at any sport – or anything in life for that matter – you have to practice and work at it! There's no way to become a great shooter other than to get in the gym and shoot over, and over, and over again. Then get up the next day and do the same thing over, and over, and over again. Your commitment will be directly tied to your success! And even more … have fun!"

About the Author

Gloria Riherd has a B.S. degree in elementary education and a M.S. as a reading specialist. She has been a teacher for 34 years in South Dakota. Helping children learn to read has been a lifetime passion for Gloria. She resides in Rapid City, SD, and is presently tutoring dyslexia students out of her home.

Gloria's husband, Ron, coached basketball for many years. It became their lifestyle that lasted 40 years. The couple spent a lifetime watching girls grow and develop into successful basketball players. Her favorites were their two grown daughters, Jill and Jody, who also played basketball in high school. "I encourage more girls to go for their dreams in whatever sport is their passion," she said.